THE · CLOVERDALE · PRIZE · FOR · POETRY · 1992

SHOETOWN

Poems by
Gerald McCarthy

THE · CLOVERDALE · LIBRARY

The · Cloverdale · Prize · For · Poetry · 1992

Shoetown

poems
by Gerald McCarthy

Library of Congress Catalog Card Number

92-071673

International Standard Book Number

1-55605-207-3

Printed in the United States of America

Cloverdale Corporation
Bristol, IN   46507-9460

A NOTE FROM THE PUBLISHER

The Cloverdale Library is pleased to annually sponsor *The Cloverdale Prize for Poetry*, a $5,000.00 prize to publish a major work for a first-time published poet from North America or Ireland.

Gerald McCarthy is the winner of the 1992 Cloverdale Prize for Poetry and we are pleased to release to the public a collection of his poetry. It is our intention to annually introduce writers with poetic talent in a genuine effort to both promote the writing arts and to nurture those who are singularly gifted as poets and writers.

It is a personal privilege for me to serve as the Director of the Prize and the Senior Editor of The Cloverdale Library of Modern Poetry. It is our hope that such efforts as these by the Cloverdale Corporation will be welcomed by the literary community and positively matched by the publishing community.

John H. Morgan
Publisher

ACKNOWLEDGEMENTS

Portions of this work originally appeared in *America, Ploughshares, The Beloit Poetry Journal, Poet Lore, Mid-American Review, Harbor Review, Cincinnati Poetry Review, Wisconsin Review, Road Apple Review, The And Review, Nebo,* and *Aisling.*

"For A Friend in Prison," "Against the Rain" and "The Hooded Legion" originally appeared in *TriQuarterly.*

"The Hooded Legion" also appeared in *TriQuarterly-20th Anniversary Anthology* and in *Carrying the Darkness-American Indochina: The Poetry of the Vietnam War* and *Unaccustomed Mercy: Soldier Poets of the Vietnam War* from Texas Tech University Press.

"Note in a bottle" and "Riding Fence" originally appeared in *New Letters.* "Note in a bottle" also appeared in *New Letters Reader II* and in *A Geography of Poets.*

My thanks to the New York State Council on the Arts and Creative Artists in Public Service for grants during the time I was completing some of the poems in this collection.

The epigraph from Stephen Crane is from *The Collected Poems of Stephen Crane,* edited by William Follett. New York. Alfred A. Knopf, Inc. 1956. Seventh Printing.

for my mother and father

"And long days I climbed
Through regions of pure snow.
When I had before me the summit-view,
It seemed that my labour
Had been to see gardens
Lying at impossible distances."

Stephen Crane
The Black Riders

TABLE OF CONTENTS

I

II

I

Susquehanna

Morning, a rose colored blush
against the windshield.

The names of small towns
drift past.
The route sign fades,
a white hand waving
twelve more miles.

Now I know the way.
The years scatter like a shower
of sparks in the rear-view mirror.

*

Shadow, the greenskeep,
leans out over his mower
and calls my name.

I lift the steel pin,
push open the wire gate.
The tractor jerks ahead,
a clumsy moth shredding sunlight
into its canvas wings.

I watch it cross the morning
fairways. He showed me
the river nettles that caused a rash,
chokeweed, knotweed, and toothworts.

*

The humpback Dodge is a blur
in the glass storefronts.
My father turns the wheel
to the right, hands straining
against his anger.

He leads me back to the field,
lets me fight all five of the boys
in turn. As long as it's fair, he yells,
and pushes me forward.

I hold on to the rail
and he goes down again.
I can see his eyes open,
his hand grabbing my hair
and pulling me under.

*

The mist clings like smoke,
a haze along the river's edge.
I remember the campfires of August,
nightfishing near the pumping house.

I cross the steel bridge
above the creek,
where the golf course stretches out
like a green dream of summer.

Blue road, blue shadows...
On the river, the carp
begin to jump
in the first rush of sunlight.

283

Past the rows of Hollyhocks,
the barbed wire choked with chicory,
pale blue in the sun,
she pulled me down into the field
and I promised, promised knowing
I had to go away.

I don't know how many years
it's been. The truck backs up,
the concrete tumbles down the chute.
Sweating, bare to the waist,
Frank and I shoveled it all out.

Each night we tried to face each other,
gave in to the tiredness:
our own reflections beyond the row
of bottles.

She said: The world wasn't built
in a day, you know. I thought
I knew. How much time each stone
took to set, how each day the cement hardened,
the skin bleached with lime.

*

Sully let the Chevy wind out in third,
hitting the hill's crest at eighty,
the car sliding sideways
bottoming-out in the stones.

Later, shooting pool in town,
he jacked his weight to one leg
and asked if I thought I'd ever
get out.

Fifty-forty, he said. You spot,
I break. A fair chance.
I can see the taillights,
the back-up bells coming on.

He stands with a beer in his hand,
yells he'll take on the whole place.
Louder now, I can hear his voice.
He calls and calls, but I'll never
reach him in time.

Note in a bottle

The Erie-Lackawanna trains are the ghosts
of summer nights. A town of freight yards,
tanning factories, timeclocks.
A town that smelled like leather.

I walk the ties through yards
and loading docks, remember
crawling between rails,
watching the headlights of sheriff cars.

If I listen I can almost hear the sirens,
glimpse the smudge of orange sky
beyond the smokestacks.
I push open the door to Ernie's Grill
on the North Side of town, the Italian side.
His hands stained brown from shoe dye,
John Robinsky cursed the heat, swore
the union would never get in.

It never did. They quit making leather
from cowhide. They closed the factories,
laid-off the workers.

Robinsky raised pigeons because it was
something he could do.
We used to watch them lift off
and carry those messages away.

Nobody answered, John. No one heard
anything but that flapping of wings.
The gun lifted, the glass raised.

Soot filled years in the attic
with the wire cages.
Mornings in the steel vats,
the drying sheds. Nobody counted.

A town of mortgages, parking lots.
I turn away, walk home
toward my father's house,
toward a light in the window
of an upstairs room,
that flickers and goes out.

Tannery, 1945

Boots, boots,
boots for soldiers.
Dress boots and combat boots,
black leather, brown leather,
hooks instead of eyelets,
eyelets instead of hooks.
Boots with straps and buckles,
boots with nylon laces.

Watch out! This way!
The hides are coming,
piles stacked on pallets,
loaded off railroad cars.
What welt? What dye?
The vats are full.

Boots, moving off
to armies, marching,
kicking cadence
stomping the icy ground.
Legless boots
filled with blood.
One pair for the foreman's brother,
one for the dyer's son.

Marching boots, coming
back, scuffed and heelless.
Shuffling, limping,
lined up against the rail.
Boots in the closet, in the attic,
molding in the cellarway.
Boots for the junkman,
The Salvation Army,
boots for the poor, the forgotten,
thrown on the garbage heap.

Rangoon, 1944

After the engines caught fire
the pilot held it nose up
and you bailed out——
a line of stick men
falling into the bamboo grass.
The co-pilot broke his leg
and you carried him for six days
through the monsoon.
You turned
from my bed after you'd told it,
and before you let the dark in
all around us, stared
your hands on the open doorway.
As if for those few moments
you were above it all again——
the house on West Main, the factory
downtown.
As if standing there
another life still held——
spreading like the blossoms of parachutes
above a deep green sea.

Nanticoke

The creek has furrowed
from the summer's day
we swam nude beneath the trestle,
the railroad tracks have heaved
like gnarled iron roots.
Sirens broke the afternoon
that day the state police
chased a prisoner through the bottomland,
and for the first time
we grew afraid of our nakedness,
the attraction to each other's bodies.
Nights I lay awake
imagined him
stumbling on the rocks
along the brackish backwater,
the lights circling,
forcing him in.
But all I heard were the freights
slowing for the West Endicott yards,
the cicadas out along the field's edge.
I wonder what became of him,
that stranger they chased into the river.
The switching shack is gone
swept away in spring flood.
One by one the factories closed
the trains stopped coming,
now gangs of boys toss stones
through the black windows of empty warehouses.

Island Lake

The dirt road ends in blackberry thicket
an outcrop of stone——highrock
the Cayuga called it.

Through the evergreens, the silver maple,
the birch, six lakes like drops of blue mist,
each one a mirror.

*

We stared at the planes
through the stereo viewer
until we were blind with silver,
my brother straddling
the rail, his face
pushed up against my own.

A wall to the roar of engines,
a small hole in the future.
And how many more years to know
the thrust, the lift off?

There is a platform
crowded with faces, a window
opening like the shutter of a camera.

And the fields become one field,
layer on layer, one glimpse
among many.

*

My uncle cracks his knuckles
and stares at his hands——piecework,
he says, shaking his head.

Laid-off from Fisher Body in Flint,
he's come east to package shoes.

His days off he climbs out of the valley
hunting for mushrooms in the hedgerows.

He showed me how to cross the open places,
to ease down the creek bank to find the ones
that were good to eat.

Later, we washed them in the well sink,
the white caps bobbing in the tub,
his hands pushing their tiny heads under.

*

TJ smiles and says the legion boys
are buying.

All through the afternoon we worked,
setting the forms for the feed mill.

At night we'd drink in the small-town bars,
shooting eight ball until it was too late
to do anything but sleep.

The five a.m. wake-ups, the foreman yelling:
let's go, let's pour it out.

A dream of Friday nights, of dollars
slid across copper-topped counters.

*

Far below a boat casts off,
its ripples widening.

My grandfather leans forward
his forehead wrinkles,
his thick fingers slip the hook
into the waterbeetle
as he lets the line spin out—
blue nylon circles arcing
above the water.

And drawing close
he whispers: watch,
watch how they rise to it.

*

My brother calls from the backyard—
the shadows of a church, of a time
I said I was sorry and meant it.

He calls, but now I cannot hear him,
and we are running side by side
as if to outrun even memory itself.

As if we could outdistance
the smokestacks, the vacant lots,
the VA homes.
And in some hollow on the cliffs,
share the afternoon, the blur of traffic
from the world below, crawling
like a terrible chameleon,
calling us both away.

Children of the dust

"and all my days are trances"
                    Poe

Well gentlemen, they said,
we take the first three dreams you have
and call them memory—
you never dream anything else.

Flashing on and off
the corridors tilt sideways
and slide away.

We sit, staring at the new arrivals—
a shuffle of feet, stale air,
cigarette smoke.
We wait for mail call, lunch call,
medication.
Everyone takes his turn.

The morning we found Curtis,
I woke to the nurse's scream,
an odor of chlorine and steel
a corpsman yelling about the blood.

Later, I learned he'd cut his way out
with a butter knife
after the last bedcheck at four a.m.

*

There were other voices
newer dreams
as we stared at the shipyards
through the wire gratings,
sunlight and the deeper blue
of the sea.

The night I held Glen in my arms
because he couldn't stop shaking,
I could feel it run through me
as he whispered——everything
is turning away.

He smiled as they strapped him down,
hit him with the shot of thorazine.
Pale moths fluttered in rooms
bleached white, shadows fell
like wet leaves.

That night
when the nurse doled out
the sleeping tabs,
no one spoke.
But we knew as the metal taste
left us numb, listless,
all the ways out were the same.

*

And the night, the night
we had names for, its breath
was our breath, the long sweep
of oncoming wave, a sigh
lulling us with promises.

We called it friend, brother,
because sleep tricked us
like a sorrow with one eye.

And we called, called until
there was nothing left
except a single black wing
hovering above a grassy place,
and the dead were lined up—
their names all the places
that were us.

And we lingered, staring
as the faces blurred,
became the pale blossoms
of cupped cigarettes, pages
torn from an album,
curled with turning.

*

Already the trembling begins,
as if the last light at the windows
brought it on, the light
spilling in from the salt marsh,
up from the docks,
the gut bars of sailor town.

A light that in its rush
caught up the fears of all
who drifted with it,
as if the past were in it,
causing the jackhammer crew
to look up from their work.
As if the new spring were buried
in the light, and this long tattoo
could rise like a lyre
above the narcotic American dusk.

Here I Am

I came back, I said
to my friends, my brother
hiding in an upstairs room,
my father hurrying off to work.
Relax, they said, take it easy,
I said it so many times
they turned away.
I told a priest in a dark booth
and he made the sign of the cross.
I came up to strangers
and told them: hey, it's me,
I'm here——home at last.
So what, they said, what's new?
I talked to bartenders, old men,
jazzed out diddy-boppers.
They looked at me as if to ask,
what's wrong?
I whispered to the starched
khaki shirts in my closet,
I called to the shoes,
black shiny ones from high school,
old running shoes, brown snap-ups
from confirmation.
Hey, I said, it's me.
I said, listen,
but they kept right on.
I ran naked through night fields
lay spreadeagled in the corn.
Here, I said, here I am.
But all I heard
was the rustling of the dry stalks.

The End of the World, etc.

I would like to take it all back,
this suit doesn't belong to me.
I'm the undercover man, an agent
transferred to a far district.

If I listen to the singer
it's a state of mind, a mask we put on
until the fire comes.

The people I meet keep getting stranger.
They buy bonds and new cars,
fall over themselves on the way to the bank.

I feel like I'm a secret.
My life becomes a series of documents
shuffled by men at steel desks.

Look, the esophagus is a place
of mistrust.
It must be Sunday, I feel like a priest.

For A Friend in Prison

Today the newspaper headlines—
New Death Penalty Bill Approved.

A letter on the table—
an extended sentence, a new bid
upstate. I see your face
behind the pages.

I hear the gate guard
cough and shake his keys
loose. A voice says:
one, coming in.

The electric door
slides shut.
After shackling your hands and ankles,
the guards lead you down a tunnel
toward the D block cell.

An afternoon sun
breaks through bare trees,
passes over some cut yellow flowers
on a window ledge.

Riding Fence

This would be the day I asked
for forgiveness and found the counter girl
in pigtails. The sign flashes:
time and temperature.

I wonder if I can continue to measure
each day like this. Half a glass,
half a glass, onward.

This would be a way of asking
how much, and not hearing anything.
Silence, she wrote
is a white fur glove in the snow.

Oh anyone, anyone. Silence is the steam
rising, the word half-finished.

This would be the hour of silence,
this unfilmed episode of gray dawn.

Graywood

Friday, strong wind
through bare trees.
Something is wrong in the sky.

I wake like the leaf still caught
in the birch tree——afraid to stay,
afraid to let go.

A junco wavers on a broken limb,
puff of white eiderdown.
The evergreen throws ticks of seed
into the patches of snow.

No one knows me. I'm wearing a coat
of clouds and blue sky.
My pockets are torn.

Ghosts

I don't know
where it is you have gone,
what street, what prison cell,
what solitary room you call
your own. Or if you lie
unmourned, somewhere
in a city graveyard,
and restless, haunt the alleyways
the late night eateries,
wondering what went wrong.
Each year in autumn
I think I see you,
when the first leaves
begin to fall
and the streets are wet with rain.
I see you poised like some graceful crane
against a parking meter—
your dungaree leg pinned up,
your back to the traffic,
the driver's stares.
Yet, each time
as I reach out to touch
your shoulder, it's some other man
who turns grinning, hawklike,
and extends his hand,
proffering a bunch of paper flowers
each one like a tiny flame
twisted from a string of flames.
And holding that bit of redness
in my hands, one red poppy
with its scrap of flag,
I know I'll never really find you,
dark brother from another time.

And I know these odd, misshapen things
which come back, clamoring to be heard
are only the long gray lines
of a decade, indifferent to time.

The Hooded Legion

"let us put up a monument to the lie"
                    Joseph Brodsky

There are no words here
to witness why we fought,
who sent us or what we hoped to gain.

There is only the rain
as it streaks the black stone,
these memories of rain
that come back to us—
a hooded legion reflected in a wall.

Tonight we wander weaponless and cold
along the shores of the Potomac
like other soldiers who camped here
looking out over smoldering fires into the night.

What did we dream of
the summer before we went away?
What leaf did not go silver
in the last light?
What hand did not turn us aside?

Against the Rain

for Sharif, Jimmy Z., Fitz and Sonny

This morning
a meadowlark in the poplars
against the rain that rises
and disappears. I remember
asking: where will I go?
how far is it?

Today is the Fourth of July,
the flags are hung from porches,
the bells ring out their own cadence.
Ray Chunn grabs my arm in the prison hallway
after his two months in *the box*.

He says we feel the same anger
and each of us has lost.
I think of the others, nothing
ahead of them but time——inside.

I drive home, listen to the weather report,
the weekend traffic toll.
The noise of fireworks catches me offguard.
I feel trapped like the deer in an open field,
the wind bringing on the night thunder,
a ragged flare of lightning along the Marrowback.

This memory is of smoke, of the yard
littered with a world turned over,
a stain that keeps spreading into all the pictures,
wounds that will not heal.

Those who have gone away with the fire
do not come back.

Migrant Labor Camp #6

No one knows
where the day goes,
but someone is counting
bushels of cabbages
stacked in wooden crates.
They pile up like the pale
heads of another dead,
on their way to cities,
canning factories,
shopping carts.
No news is good news,
he says, shaking his head.
The gas heat swells
the cubicle, yellowing
everything in a false dawn.
And I see his eyes
as he passes me the bottle,
pushes me——
no, but I heard Lady sing
once, he says.
Nothing will bring back
the day, not this smoke
or the tinny scrape
of the wind
flapping the plastic windowpane.

Mary

She laughs at the screen,
the figures float away in blue haze.
At lunch she talks of the coal mines
and my grandfather moves through the half-light.

But now it is a cave she comes to,
a tunnel of black smoke, and her voice
rises, trills. She is a girl of six
afraid of the night sky closing,
surrounding the terraced hills.

She answers across the miles
of connections, but does not know me.
She works on black leather uppers
in the factory, walks home with her sisters
through knee high drifts.

And now there are other voices,
rooms she does not know.
She folds white towels end to end,
presses them smooth on a steel table,
stares at the screen and giggles.

Tonight she will not eat or sleep.
She paces the floor, climbs the stair,
clicks the light on as she goes,
mumbling about the moon, the boarders
getting up for work.

Frankie

Each day he descends
into those caves of ice,
and the dark creeps in over him
as the cars roll down the shaft.
Later, older, he rises
the cars loaded with their milky diamonds.
He surfaces to the tarpaulined piles,
great pyramids of salt glow darkly
against a winter sky.
He passes the towns whose names
cling like bad luck and loss——
Pike and Trout and Nunda.
Until it seems he's gone in circles
and the roadhouses are a blur
of steamy windowpanes, riding
the edge, he'd say, the headlights
calling up all the days of work
and forgetting.

The Arc Welder

He lifts his hand
and the thin seam of light
moves with him, the glow
scatters a shower of sparks
like gold dust upon the wooden floor.
And with one motion
he makes the harrow
whole again.
The tractor moves,
the earth pushes up.
He turns his back
to the fields, to the farmer
hunched over the gears,
plowing the furrows in the dusk.
There is only the darkened shop,
the light feeding in through the open door,
and his daughter's voice outside
rising in play.
His back to the light,
hands gripping the iron bar,
he says: I know
she wants me home, but this wheel
won't wait, and grinning
he flips the spark guard down,
lighting the torch.
I see him still
as the evening settles,
his shop door open to the chill,
the motor whirring amidst
an amber glow of sparks, alone
he turns the wheel in his hands.

for John Kellog

IV

Smoke

"Mi corazón no puede con la carga"
                    Hernandez

Is it the snow
blurring the letters,
the snow drifting
like a line of gray clouds
among the markers?
It does not stop.
And I know I've come back again
as if your name in stone
could bring more than this breath
this blur of something moving,
your shadow so late at night
coming for me.
Once, in Sintra
in a stone parapet,
I heard the notes of a flute
rise in the air,
and startled, thinking
I was alone there,
I turned to see two lovers
descending the stone stair,
one dark, the other fair.
They did not notice me,
and as the evening sea came in
I dreamt of you, your silver fingers
turned to water, air.
We must have dreamed together
you and I, I remember
my fingers touching your dark hair,
the snow filling up the backyards,
the first cold flakes on my mouth.
Oh, I have gone asking for you,
embracing what I could

as the first green deepened
the still fields.
No, it's not the snow
drifting here among the stones,
only the smoke from the caretaker's fire
as he burns last fall's leaves
along the iron fence.

for my mother, Marie
(1913-1951)

Flag Burning
(a Prayer)

The Sherente of South America
believe the stars
are their dead children
who have climbed into the sky.
Let each star
be a hundred children,
a thousand.
Let their innocence
keep rising above us
so we may remember
who we are, how we came here.
Let the clear cold air
be filled with them,
because the names have fallen
off the old pictures now,
and the newsreels have faded.
As another autumn
turns toward winter,
and we pause to look skyward,
hoping to glimpse Orion's belt
or Cassiopeia,
let us pray to remember
these lies we've lived with
for so long in such earnest.

At the crossroads

This is where the children fell.
See how the dust absorbs them,
how the flies rise in slow circle
tracing the outline of their lives.

This is where the mother
kneeling in the scrub grass,
pressed her palms to the earth.

Listen, you can still hear her sigh.
Not the sound of the wind
although the wind carries it.
Not the noise of a train passing
in the late afternoon sun
although the train echoes it.

Her cries keep coming back
across the field, lingering
in the withered leaves, the dry,
forgotten places.

As easy as morning

Your hair was black then
a dark river streaming
upon the sheets,
and you said
you wanted love
to be as easy
as morning,
something that comes
and never leaves.
I stared at your eyes
their color changing
from deep green
to aquamarine,
and it seemed we held
the night in our hands.
You turned to me
in your sleep
and I held you here
in my arms
as the light
in your dark hair
went on shining.

To the screech owl

Tonight I listen to your call
rising dolorous
out of the damp creek bottom,
and I know it's you again—
the lonely one who passes in June
heading south to the Delaware,
the open marshes of the sea.
You, searching for a familiar cry
in answer, here beneath the tulip poplars.
You, the one who calls,
yet never enters, never stays.
Like the calm after the rain
ceases, the hush of your too human voice,
alone on the wing.

Threnody

So this is the street,
I should have recognized it
by now, known it would come
to this——a ragged orchard
and the leaves falling,
the dusk stretching its nets
over the brown fields.
The heart calling
moon, November moon,
come out, give me some light
again, show me the road
winding like a bright scarf
through the mountains,
the thistle edging
the hill's crest, the trail
leading away from here.
Oh moon, etch it slowly
for me. Call back
your song from the meadow,
the voice murmuring
a name, and your light
your light coming through.

Sudden snow, sudden moment
of grace,
let the wind come on
carrying the mist
and the sleet,
let it shake the branches
of the pine
and settle in the eyesockets
of a deer's skull
wedged atop the stone wall,
so that the vines grew
around it, and held it down.

Oh come on snow,
you can do better than that.
Cover up the grape vines
and the ivy,
rime the wings
of the barred owl
as it hunts the creek bottom.
Cover the stalks of wild phlox,
of knapweed and lupine
and what was once
some purple loosestrife.

Bring down your chill
and choke the roadside stream,
cut loose along the ridgeline
and let me see you.
Oh shadow, shadow paler
than this heart
calling out for cold
and distance
and the gathering cloud,
show yourself in the clearing
and let me walk through you,
as if you were smoke
or the chalky wings of butterflies.
Let me sit beside you
until my breath is yours,
and I am nothing
no one.

ABOUT THE AUTHOR

Gerald McCarthy was born in Endicott, New York, in 1947. A Vietnam Veteran, he worked as a stone cutter and concrete finisher before attending the Writers Workshop at The University of Iowa. His poetry has appeared in numerous magazines and anthologies. Currently, he teaches writing and literature at St. Thomas Aquinas College.